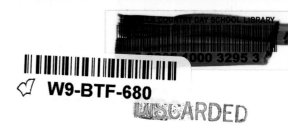
DATE DUE

	FEB 22 2017		

DEMCO 38-296

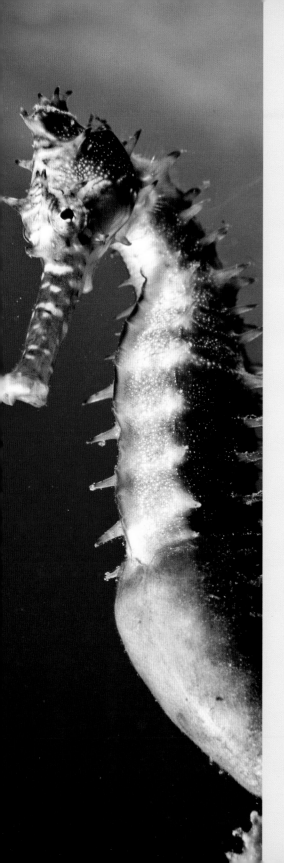

Project Seahorse

A Barbigant's seahorse in Anilao in the northern Philippines.

Project Seahorse

By Pamela S. Turner

Photographs by Scott Tuason

Houghton Mifflin Harcourt

Boston   New York

For the children of Jandayan Island —Pamela S. Turner

For my brother Christopher —Scott Tuason

For information about permission to reproduce selections from this book, write to Permissions, Houghton Mifflin Harcourt Publishing Company, 215 Park Avenue South, New York, New York 10003.

www.hmhco.com

The text of this book is set in Scala LF.

The Library of Congress has cataloged the hardcover edition as follows:
Turner, Pamela S.
  Project Seahorse / by Pamela S. Turner.
    p. cm. — (Scientists in the field)
  1. Sea horses—Juvenile literature. I. Title.
  QL638.S9T87 2010
  597'.6798—dc22
                  2009049707

ISBN: 978-0-547-20713-1 hardcover
ISBN: 978-0-544-22580-0 paperback

Printed in China/ SCP 10987654321

4500521222

CONTENTS

Amanda Vincent measures a tiger tail seahorse while Heather Koldewey records the data.

CHAPTER ONE

A Night on the Reef

A dive light shines through the midnight water. It passes over crusty coral, rough rock, and smooth sand. Crabs scuttle sideways and vanish; navy blue sea urchins wave fat spines. Where are the fish? A bit of green, bright as an emerald, gives away a wrasse's hiding place. The fish is asleep in a crevice.

Amanda Vincent and Heather Koldewey are scuba-diving in the water just off Handumon (Han-DOO-mon), a small village on an island in the Philippines. They sweep their dive lights back and forth over the reef, looking for tiger tail seahorses. The scientists must search at night because during the day tiger tail seahorses hide in holes and crevices in the reef. As night falls tiger tail seahorses come out to feed. Seahorses use their toothless snouts like little vacuum cleaners,

A pregnant male tiger tail seahorse clings to a branch of acropora coral. Each little "bud" on the coral is a tiny animal—a coral polyp.

sucking small prey (such as tiny shrimp) from the water and swallowing the food whole. Even when seahorses emerge from their hiding places they are difficult to spot. The animals look like just another branch of coral.

There! That looks *almost* like a coral knob. But not quite. Black button eyes give the seahorse away.

Amanda gently unfurls the seahorse's monkey-like tail and cradles the fish in her hand. Its texture alternates between nubby ridges and stretchy-soft skin. From the seahorse's shape Amanda can tell that this one is a male. He curls his tail tightly around Amanda's finger. There is no expression on his horsey face, but one of the seahorse's eyes settles on Amanda. His other eye rolls around, completely independently, to watch Heather. Heather takes notes as Amanda measures the seahorse's trunk and tail.

When the scientists are finished, Amanda returns the seahorse to his holdfast (the place the seahorse grabs with his tail). It doesn't take long to find the seahorse's mate. Her tail clutches a nearby coral branch. After measuring the female seahorse, Amanda and Heather swim away. Their dive lights flicker over the reef as they search for more seahorses.

Rodrigo "Digoy" Paden swims the reef at night, too. Instead of a dive light, Digoy mounts a kerosene lantern on the front of his paddleboat. The lantern shines down through the shallow water and lights up the reef below. Digoy pulls the boat along with a rope held in one hand. Instead of using scuba tanks, Digoy holds his breath when he dives. And when Digoy dives he usually finds something. He's been fishing since he was fifteen. His dad fished, and so did his grandfather.

Digoy swims over a wide circle of bare rock and rubble. This is what remains after "blast-fishing." A few years ago a fisher dropped a homemade bomb (often made from fertilizer packed in a sardine tin) into the water. The explosion killed everything within a wide circle, even animals nobody eats. Many sank to the bottom. Some floppy fish bobbed to the surface, every bone in their body shattered by the blast's shock wave. The blast-fisher scooped up the dead fish. Now only this circle of dead coral remains. It will take at least five years, and perhaps decades, for the coral in this spot to grow back.

Live coral is a community of many tiny coral polyps living together. Each coral polyp is a tiny animal that captures even tinier plants and animals by filtering them from the water. Polyps also get energy from the sun (courtesy of photosynthesizing algae that live with the polyps). Coral polyps secrete chemicals that harden into a skeleton. These skeletons, with their thin skin of living polyps, make up coral reefs. Coral reefs are the largest living structures on earth, and

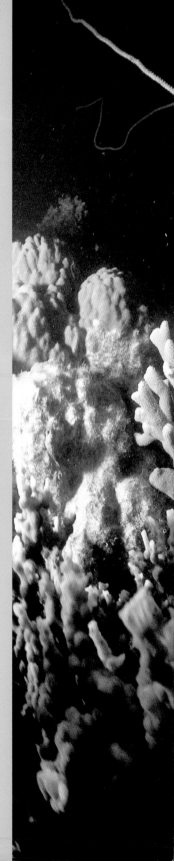

Rodrigo "Digoy" Paden searches the reef.

home to thousands of other species. When coral reefs are destroyed, many creatures have no place to live.

Digoy swims away from the dead, blasted area to another part of the reef. Coral clusters along the bottom, full of ridges, twists, and branches—fine places for reef creatures to live and grow. Below Digoy, a seahorse sways with the gentle rise and fall of the sea swells. A snorkeling tourist would probably think the seahorse is just another knob of coral. Even a trained biologist might not see the fish. But Digoy spots it right away. He swims down and cups the seahorse in his hand.

This reef is home to countless animals like the odd and lovely seahorse. For many people in Handumon, including Digoy, this reef is not just a beautiful place. It's the source of their livelihood. By collecting this seahorse and selling it, Digoy can earn money. Dried seahorses are used in traditional Chinese medicine, and many people in Europe, North America, and other countries buy curios made from dried seahorses and purchase living seahorses for aquariums. Selling this seahorse could help provide rice for Digoy's dinner table and school uniforms for his children.

Digoy opens his hand. The seahorse sinks down and links its tail around its holdfast.

Not every fisher is willing to make this kind of sacrifice. Many still collect seahorses. There are fewer seahorses on this reef than there used to be because too many have been taken from the sea. Overfishing is a problem not just for seahorses but for many other kinds of fish. Some of the fish feed local families, while other fish are shipped away to distant markets. Most large fish on this reef have already been caught; the fish that remain are small. And blast-fishing is still going on.

Handumon's problems aren't unique. Many coral reefs around the world face similar threats. How can reefs be protected, along with the livelihood of people like Digoy? Finding solutions to this thorny problem is a main goal of Project Seahorse.

A thorny seahorse in Anilao, northern Philippines. Crabs, large fish, and rays sometimes eat seahorses, but most predators don't like the seahorse's spiky, bony body.

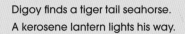

Digoy finds a tiger tail seahorse. A kerosene lantern lights his way.

There are more different coral species in the Philippines than in any other country. Unfortunately, even beautiful reefs like this one (Anilao in the northern Philippines) are threatened by human activities.

A Barbigant's seahorse clings to a sea fan on a reef in the northern Philippines. This cashew-size seahorse is one of the world's smallest. Like many seahorses, it can change color to match its surroundings.

CHAPTER TWO

Mr. Mom

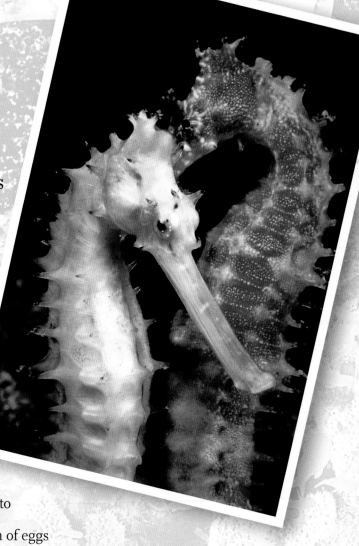

The male seahorse's brood pouch bulges like a balloon. It puffs in and out, in and out, like the cheeks of a trumpet player. The seahorse pumps with his tail, bending and folding like jacknife, working hard to give birth. A squirt, a gush—two babies pop out. Each is a tiny, perfect copy of its father. Soon a little cluster of brothers and sisters appears in the water. A few of the baby seahorses cling to Dad, but this family gathering doesn't last long. One by one the young seahorses swim away.

The mother seahorse waits nearby. She does nothing to help the father or the babies. Soon she'll have a new batch of eggs ready to deposit into her mate's brood pouch.

13

Baby White's seahorses cling to seagrasses. Baby seahorses are on their own from the moment they are born.

Depending on the species, a seahorse father's pregnancy lasts between nine and forty-five days, and between five and two thousand babies may nestle in his pouch. Dad isn't just babysitting, either. He supplies his offspring with the oxygen and nutrients they need to grow. And the fluid inside his pouch changes as his youngsters develop. It becomes saltier and saltier. By the time his babies are born, the fluid in Dad's pouch is just like seawater. When his little ones pop out they will feel right at home in the sea.

Amanda Vincent was drawn to seahorses by their oddball biology. Although she was born in Canada, Amanda spent much of her childhood in South America. She credits family camping trips for nurturing her love of the outdoors, especially the ocean. When Amanda was a high school student, she had planned to study politics and languages in college. "I managed to avoid science until my last year in high school," says Amanda. "But then my biology teacher really inspired me."

During graduate school Amanda decided to combine her two interests—the ocean and the origin of sex differences—by studying seahorses. And Amanda would be a pioneer. No biologist had ever studied seahorses in the wild.

Over the next four years Amanda spent hundreds of hours underwater in Florida and Australia, studying seahorse reproduction. Seahorse courtship dances might last for many hours, the male and female twirling around a common holdfast. The couple's skins would turn pale, then dark again. Sometimes the fish swam with tails entwined as if holding hands. Finally, the pair would rise in the water and join belly to belly as the female placed her eggs in the male's pouch. Then both would sink back to grasp a holdfast and sway with the passing current. Amanda discovered that most seahorses mate for life, replaying their charming courtship ballet over and over.

Amanda still remembers a pair of White's seahorses she studied in Australia. The pregnant male was attacked during the night by another animal that bit a hole in his pouch and sucked out his babies. Amanda didn't expect the male to survive his terrible injury. Though nearby single males tried to lure the female seahorse away, she refused to abandon her wounded mate. Every morning the female greeted her partner with the courtship dance that seahorse couples use to keep their reproductive cycles in harmony. After a few months, the male's pouch healed and he fathered another brood. "For any animal, that level of devotion is extraordinary," says Amanda.

After Amanda finished her Ph.D. she turned her attention to understanding how seahorses

Baby White's seahorses cling to their father moments after birth. White's seahorses are found in the Solomon Islands and off the east coast of Australia.

15

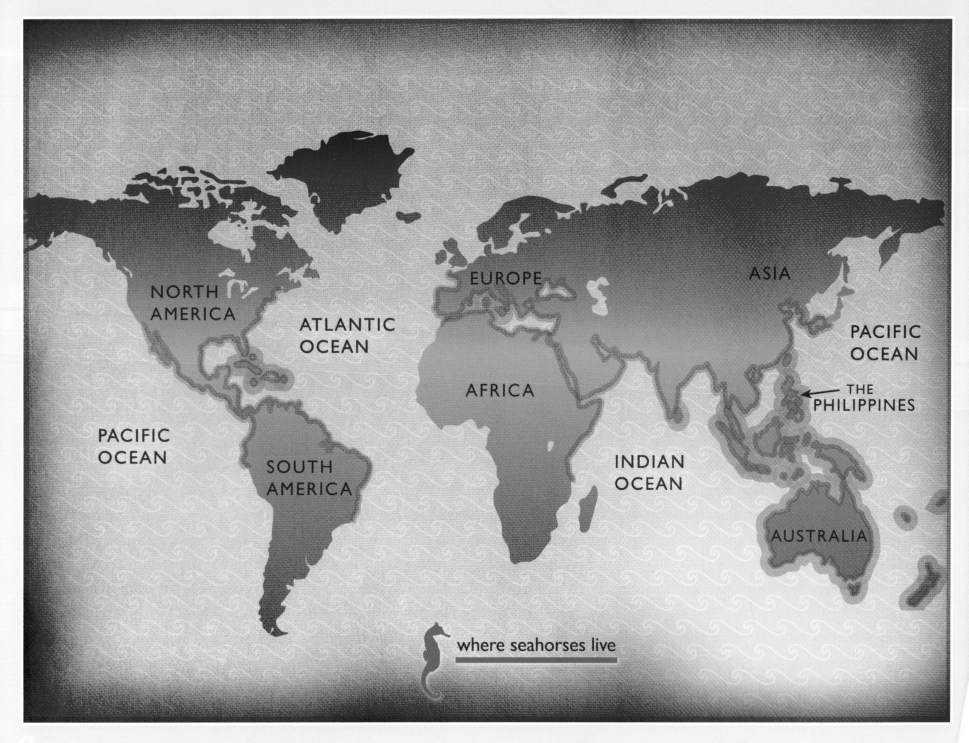

NORTH AMERICA

ATLANTIC OCEAN

EUROPE

ASIA

PACIFIC OCEAN

THE PHILIPPINES

AFRICA

PACIFIC OCEAN

SOUTH AMERICA

INDIAN OCEAN

AUSTRALIA

where seahorses live

At least forty species of seahorses live in the world's tropical (warm water near the equator) and temperate (water neither warm nor extremely cold) seas. The biggest seahorse is the banana-size big belly seahorse, and the smallest is the pinenut-size Denise's pygmy seahorse. Scientists know very little about some species of seahorses. They do know that many species are in trouble.

were coping with being fished and traded. The clues she followed led her to the Philippines, which was selling many seahorses to other countries. When Amanda and her Filipino partners began exploring the country's fisheries, they discovered that a great many seahorses were being caught along Danajon (Da-NA-hon) Bank. Danajon Bank is a double reef arching like a crown over the northern coast of Bohol, a large island in the central Philippines. Amanda calls the almost eighty-four-mile-long (135-kilometer) Danajon Bank "a rare jewel." Only six double reefs exist in the entire world.

The jewel, however, was losing its shine. Far too much marine life was being removed, often in very damaging ways. As the human population along Danajon Bank grew, so did demand for food and other resources. Every day blast-fishing tore away more and more of the reef. Fish and shrimp farming ponds replaced vital stands of mangrove trees. Dredging and pollution destroyed seagrasses. These three habitats—coral reefs, mangroves, and seagrasses—are closely linked. Many coral reef creatures spend part of their lives in seagrasses or mangroves. If one part of this ecosystem suffers, all parts suffer.

Amanda and her Filipino colleagues talked to political leaders, shopkeepers, teachers, seahorse traders, seaweed farmers, rice farmers, and of course many fishers, including Digoy Paden. They discovered that people all over the Philippines were worried about the health of marine habitats. In particular, they found out that seahorse populations were in trouble. The older fishers said they were now catching fewer seahorses and other fish, and the fish they did catch were small. Many fishers were also unhappy with blast-fishing and other bad fishing practices such as bottom trawling (towing a large fishing net along the ocean floor behind one or more boats). They could see the damage to the reefs with their own eyes.

Amanda spoke to people in many other Southeast Asian countries. It was the same all over: lots of people wanted to buy seahorses, but there were fewer and fewer seahorses to catch. By investigating the trade in dozens of countries, Amanda found that about twenty million seahorses were caught every year. Most came from Thailand, Vietnam, India, and the Philippines. Most went to China for use in traditional Chinese medicines. In addition, many thousands of seahorses became curios such as key chains and paperweights. And vast numbers were also sold live for public and home aquariums. Most would

Heather and Amanda with one of Project Seahorse's outrigger boats (called a *banca* in the Philippines)

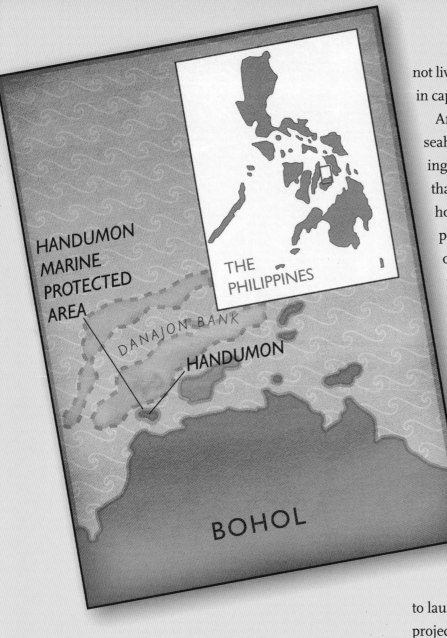

HANDUMON
MARINE
PROTECTED
AREA

THE
PHILIPPINES

DANAJON BANK

HANDUMON

BOHOL

About 96 million Filipinos live on 4,000 of the 7,107 islands in the Philippines. Many of the poorest people in the Philippines are dependent on fish for the protein they need. Beef, pork, and chicken are too expensive.

not live long; seahorses are very difficult to keep in captivity.

Amanda's data showed that in some places seahorses were in real trouble. By interviewing fishers and traders, Amanda estimated that over a ten-year period (1985–95) seahorse catches in the Philippines fell by 75 percent. From her studies of seahorse biology, Amanda knew that the animals could not recover quickly from overfishing. Seahorses have small surviving broods compared with other fish. They also spend lots of time and energy finding and bonding with a mate. If a seahorse loses its mate it must find another unattached partner before it can breed again. Yet seahorses like to stay in their home area rather than swim long distances searching for a new mate.

Clearly, seahorses needed help.

In 1994, Amanda and a Philippine environmental organization joined forces to launch the world's first seahorse conservation project. A few years later, Heather Koldewey, who was studying seahorse genetics in England, helped Amanda create Project Seahorse. Through science, education, and community action, they hoped to bring some luster back to Danajon Bank—the Philippines' damaged jewel.

Project Seahorse scientists often help identify newly discovered seahorse species, such as these Pontoh's pygmy seahorses in Raja Ampat, Indonesia.

How the Seahorse Got His Pouch

Seahorses are weird. The pony-faced fish don't have scales; instead they wear a suit of flexible armor. Seahorses hover and flutter rather than swimming in normal fishy fashion. They don't have tail fins at all. Instead, they use a strong fin on their back for power, and steer with small fins on either side of their head. When a seahorse stops to grasp a bit of coral or a blade of seagrass, it reaches out with a monkey-like tail. How did the male's kangaroo-like pouch get added to this list of oddities?

In mammals, females usually shoulder most of the burden of caring for the young. After all, young mammals can't survive without mother's milk. But baby fish don't have the same needs as baby mammals. Fish do things differently. In many fish species the female just lays her eggs in a nest and swims off. She's done. In some species, the father fish stays behind to fertilize the eggs and guard them from predators. He may

A male White's seahorse giving birth.

also entice another female to lay her eggs in his nest. By putting all his eggs in one basket (so to speak) a male can produce the most young for the least effort. If another male fish manages to dart into the nest at the right time, the intruder may be able to fertilize some of the eggs. This deadbeat dad will become a father without investing his time and energy in daddy daycare. The male seahorse, however, doesn't have to worry about some sneaky rival fertilizing his mate's eggs. By fertilizing the eggs inside his *own* pouch, he knows all the babies will be his.

Hints about how the male pouch evolved come from the several hundred species of pipefish. Pipefish and seahorses are closely related—in fact, the seahorse is really a curled pipefish. By looking at different species of pipefish, scientists can unravel how paternal care in this group

A trio of pipefish in Papua New Guinea.

of fish evolved into something more and more specialized. In the simplest form, the male straight-nosed pipefish secretes a gluey chemical that allows his mate's eggs to stick to his body. At the next level of parental care, some male pipefish stick their eggs to their bodies and have ridges on their belly or tail to protect the developing babies. Species like the broad-nosed pipefish are even more sophisticated. The male broad-nosed pipefish has a special fold of skin that entirely covers and protects the eggs glued to his body. The skin fold even "zips" up in front. In seahorses, this fully enclosed pipefish pouch has evolved into the ultimate baby carrier: a large pocket with one small, tightly controlled opening.

"You can imagine how these steps could have led to the evolution of the male seahorse's fully sealed pouch," explains Amanda. "By looking at pipefish, we can follow a trail of clues. Each more advanced form of parental care builds carefully on earlier ways to protect the developing baby seahorses."

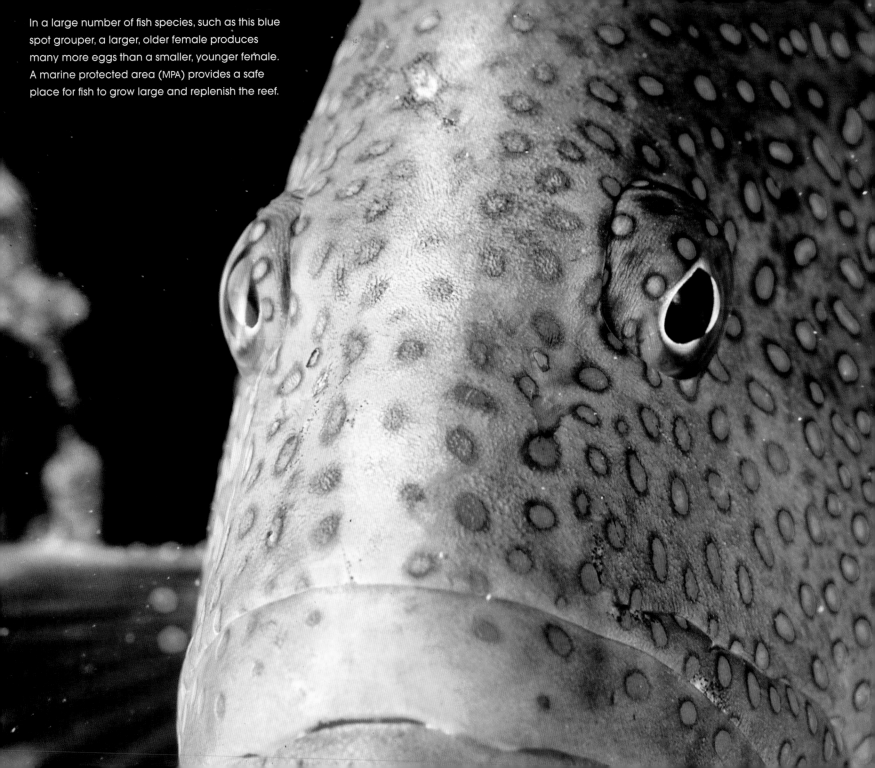

In a large number of fish species, such as this blue spot grouper, a larger, older female produces many more eggs than a smaller, younger female. A marine protected area (MPA) provides a safe place for fish to grow large and replenish the reef.

CHAPTER THREE

One Fish, Two Fish, Red Fish, Blue Fish

In a sunny day in June, it's time for one of Project Seahorse's reef surveys. Jesus Ray (J.R.) Dongallo and Mia Comeros motor across the water in a banca loaded with scuba gear and survey equipment. The outriggers are like stiff wings that balance the slender boat as it rides over the lifting, shifting swells.

J.R. grew up climbing mountains and exploring caves in Mindanao, a large island in the southern part of the Philippines. In college he became interested in marine biology and now works for Project Seahorse as a biologist. Mia is also a biologist with a keen curiosity for sea creatures and a devotion to marine conservation; she

Mia and J.R.

23

grew up with Danajon Bank as her underwater backyard. Soon she'll be leaving the Philippines to attend graduate school in the United States.

J.R. and Mia strap on their scuba gear and drop into the blue-green ocean. Muted sounds drift through the water: the *pun-pun-pun* of a distant boat engine, even the faint scratching and grinding of hundreds of little fish mouths scraping algae off the rocks and coral.

J.R. and Mia unroll a long plastic tape and lay it gently across the coral. This line is called a transect. Scientists gather data along a transect to obtain a snapshot of the reef. Data from many transects will be put together to create a portrait of this part of the reef. J.R. and Mia swim slowly along the line, recording data on an underwater writing board. How much of the transect crosses live coral? How much crosses mud or dead coral?

For the fish survey, J.R. and Mia look on either side of the yellow tape and record the species and size of nearby fish. Yellow and black butterflyfish, blue-green parrotfish, and silvery snappers glide by. A mottled brown grouper hovers over a rock. Groupers look like fat, drowsy dogs—until food appears. Then groupers become lightning fast and as ravenous as wolves. A reef with many top predators, like groupers, is a sign of a healthy coral reef. Unfortunately for groupers, people find these fish very tasty. Groupers are scarce in many parts of the Philippines because of overfishing.

Coral polyp in the Handumon MPA.

Mia records the coral cover on a transect line in Handumon's marine protected area. In 2007 Handumon's MPA was named the best MPA in the Philippines.

24

A sea slug (also called a nudibranch) in Handu-mon's marine protected area. Many sea slugs are brightly colored as a warning to predators: "Watch out, I'm poisonous!" This kind of slug is called a fried egg nudibranch. It doesn't taste like breakfast.

The white floats in front of the guard-house help mark the Handumon MPA. Handumon means "place we will remember."

J.R. and Mia's fish and coral survey is impor-tant. Ten years ago, with encouragement from Amanda and her Filipino colleagues, the people of Handumon set aside this part of the reef as a no-take marine protected area (MPA). Swim-ming, snorkeling, scuba diving, and boating are permitted. Tourists pay an entrance fee. But no fishing is allowed.

Even though no one can fish in the MPA, this no-take zone may still help local fishers (while conserving marine life). Studies in many countries have shown that fish thrive inside MPAs. MPAs have more fish and more kinds of fish. In addition, fish inside MPAs live long enough to grow big, and big fish have more off-spring. As the fish population inside an MPA grows, some of the fish "spill over" into nearby unprotected areas, where they can be caught. Setting up an MPA is like putting money in the

bank: you can get interest from the bank with-out taking out any of the original money.

When the people of Handumon created this MPA, the Project Seahorse scientists began a study of the MPA's effectiveness. Would the reef inside the MPA recover? Would the fish recover? If the reef's health did improve, how long would it take? By setting aside part of their reef, would local fishers eventually catch more fish? The Project Seahorse team is answering these questions through a series of scien-tific studies. Amanda and

Heather and Amanda measure a mangrove trunk.

On a healthy reef inside the Handumon MPA, a group of mangrove jacks swim over brain coral.

A reef off Handumon damaged by blast-fishing.

Sunlight streams through the water along the twisted trunk of an old mangrove tree. Seagrasses and mangroves are part of a larger ecosystem that includes coral reefs. Mangroves and seagrasses provide a refuge for many reef animals when they are young, small, and vulnerable.

Heather are working on one of these studies today.

As J.R. and Mia gather data along the reef, Amanda and Heather work closer to shore. Amanda and Heather stretch a yellow tape measure around a gnarled mangrove tree. This old mangrove, with its thick, twisting trunk, looks a bit like a drowned oak. But mangroves—unlike oaks and most other trees—thrive in salt water. They send their roots into the shallow, mucky border between land and sea. The young of many reef animals take shelter among the mangrove's arching roots until they are big enough to compete for food and mates out on the reef. Amanda and Heather are measuring mangrove trees to find out how fast they grow.

When J.R., Mia, Amanda, and Heather finish collecting the day's data, they head back to the Project Seahorse headquarters in Handumon. The house—built of coconut lumber, with woven bamboo walls and bamboo-strip floors—stands just a short walk from the water. The researchers transfer their raw data to a computer. When the sun sets the Project Seahorse team will get wet again—counting and measuring tiger tail seahorses.

Project Seahorse scientists have been doing surveys along Danajon Bank every year since 1998. They survey the Handumon MPA and another eight of the thirty-three MPAs that Project Seahorse has helped create on Dana-jon Bank. Areas that are not protected are also surveyed. The scientists are finding that there are more fish and more types of fish inside the Handumon MPA than outside. The fish inside the protected area are bigger than fish in unprotected areas, too. The data show that top predators such as groupers are doing especially well inside the MPA. Outside the MPA, groupers are still rare. Inside the MPA the habitat for seahorses, groupers, and other animals is gradually improving as new coral begins to grow in areas shattered by blast-fishing.

And how are the seahorses doing? Project Seahorse is using several different studies to answer this question. So far, the tiger tail surveys have not found more tiger tail seahorses inside the Handumon MPA than outside. However, the seahorses inside the protected area are bigger than those in other areas, because they survive long enough to grow large. "That's very encouraging," says Amanda. "Because bigger animals have more babies." While a younger, smaller seahorse might give birth to three hundred babies, a larger, older male can have twice as many in a brood. And research shows that the offspring of large males are more likely to grow fast and survive to adulthood. Amanda hopes that the larger broods born to the larger seahorses inside the MPA will help repopulate other parts of the reef.

Project Seahorse also estimates changes

in seahorse populations outside the MPAs by tracking both the number of seahorses caught and the effort it took to catch them. By gathering data from seahorse fishers and buyers, Project Seahorse found that seahorse catches are now about the same from year to year. Fishers from Handumon can catch quite a few seahorses from February until April, when underwater visibility is best, even though they may find no seahorses for much of the rest of the year. Project Seahorse is working with fishers to understand if MPAs are enough to keep the tiger tail seahorse populations healthy, or if fishing continues to threaten seahorses.

Project Seahorse would also like to know if there are any changes in the fish catch around MPAs. Do local fishers benefit from MPAs? The answer is very important for the future of MPAs everywhere. Yet this question is surprisingly difficult to answer, especially when studying coral reefs. Coral reef fishers use many kinds of gear to catch many kinds of fish. Fishers may also change what they do from season to season and from year to year. Measuring this type of fishing is very difficult—and measurement is the basis of science.

The Project Seahorse team often visits communities along Danajon Bank to ask villagers about their concerns, to talk about managing reefs, and to discuss research results with those who know the reef best. The biologists are accompanied by Project Seahorse community organizers, who focus on helping the people of Danajon Bank improve their lives. Exchanging information helps villagers and scientists alike make better decisions about how to use (or not use) marine resources. Danajon Bank is the villagers' home and their heritage. They want to be good stewards of the reef.

Most of the local fishers already knew a great deal about the ocean around them. But there was one thing they usually didn't know about seahorses. Mia says: "The older fishermen, they don't believe it when we say the male is the pregnant one. They say, 'No! No! It's a female!'" She laughs. "But their wives *love* the idea!"

Protected areas can help ocean wildlife, whether they are large animals such as whales or tiny animals such as this goby.

A tiger tail seahorse in the Handumon MPA.

Fish Havens

Both Amanda and Heather grew up visiting national parks with their families. In fully protected national parks, no one is allowed to shoot a deer, cut down a pine tree, dump trash, or put up a shopping mall. Most people agree that we should protect wild places, not just because we can get something in return—like a nice place to vacation—but also because it's the right thing to do.

In 1996, when Amanda and Heather began Project Seahorse, creating underwater national parks was a fairly new idea. For a long time people thought it wasn't necessary to protect the ocean. The sea is vast, isn't it? Anything dumped in it will just disappear. There are so many fish in the ocean, nobody can catch them all. Right?

That turns out to be wrong. Filipino fishers along Danajon Bank aren't the only ones trying to catch fish and coming up with fewer and fewer of them. It's happening everywhere. Overfishing has long been the ocean's biggest problem, although there are also many other threats. Scientists have discovered that fishing can do more than take too many fish out of the sea. Destructive types of fishing gear (such as trawling nets dragged across the bottom of the ocean) destroy fragile underwater habitats. Some kinds of fishing gear removes all species in their path, even the ones they didn't mean to catch, such as seahorses. Shrimp trawlers can be particularly bad, flattening the bottom and often taking nineteen pounds of other marine life for every pound of shrimp. And there is more ocean pollution, especially along coasts where many people live. Sewage turns blue water brown. Plastic bags and old fishing nets litter the shallows.

Of all the world's marine habitats, coral reefs are perhaps hit the hardest by human activities. About 10 percent of the world's population—655 million people—live within sixty-two miles (one hundred kilometers) of a coral reef. Coral can be damaged by fishing gear such as explosives or dragging nets. Sometimes people break up coral and use it as a building material. Fertilizer, pesticides, and sewage draining into the ocean can poison nearby coral, and dirt washed into the ocean can smother it.

Scientists estimate that 20 percent of all coral reefs have been destroyed by human activity, while another 35 percent of reefs are in immediate danger. And global climate change (caused by humans burning fossil fuels such as gasoline and coal) is reaching even the most remote reefs. The oceans are getting warmer, and higher water temperatures can kill coral. Climate change also puts gases in the air that eventually end up in seawater. These gases change the chemistry of seawater, increasing its acidity. Higher levels of acidity make it more difficult for corals to form their reef-building skeletons.

Now more people understand that we should take better care of the world's oceans. We shouldn't take too many fish or use destructive fishing gear. We should keep soil, pollutants, and trash out of the water. And we should reduce our use of fossil fuels.

Another thing we can do is set aside parts of the sea the same way we set aside parts of the land as national parks. This won't solve every problem, but it will keep our ocean healthier. A healthy ocean is more likely to recover

Almost 13 percent of all land on Earth is protected—but less than 1 percent of our oceans is protected.

from threats like climate change than one drowning in many problems. These special protected areas will also remind us what healthy marine habitats should look like. Otherwise, we risk thinking that our damaged oceans are normal.

Digoy searches the reef while towing
his paddleboat.

CHAPTER FOUR

At Home in Handumon

Even in the middle of the night, the tropical air is thick, soft, and warm. And noisy: the cricket chorus rising from the nearby mangroves is almost deafening. Digoy tows his small paddleboat along the reef with the line in one hand and a spear in the other. He uses one bare foot to grasp and push off the shallow coral. On the other foot Digoy wears a plywood fin.

A small filefish hides among the rocks. Digoy spears the tiny target expertly. He brings the flapping fish to the side of his boat and tosses it in. Digoy fishes from midnight until dawn. All the time Digoy is swimming, swimming, swimming. The work is exhausting. When the morning's light finally appears, Digoy heads for home.

Jenicil's third grade classroom at Handumon's elementary school.

As the insect horde falls silent, Handumon's roosters begin crowing. Digoy sorts his catch. The most valuable fish—snappers and parrot-fish—will be sold in the market so the family can buy rice, kerosene, and other necessities. Digoy's family will eat the less popular fish, like the filefish. When the fishing is bad the family will eat only rice.

Digoy's wife, Gertrudes, helps their daughters get ready for school. Fourteen-year-old Janith goes to high school. Jenicil, nine, is in third grade. Twenty-two-year-old Joel also lives at home. Eighteen-year-old Gretchen is away at college, and twenty-three-year-old Marlon works as an electrician in another town. The Paden children's success—which is quite remarkable in this very poor community—comes from Digoy and Gertrudes's firm belief in hard work and the importance of education. School awards collected by the Paden children hang by the front door, next to their father's paddling prizes. Digoy has won the local outrigger boat paddling race three years in a row.

Jenicil and Janith leave their simple home, with its small, neat garden full of purple and white orchids. Handumon is one of three villages on Jandayan Island. The villages are connected by a narrow path that is paved for most of its length. A few people ride motorcycles, but most walk like Jenicil and Janith. Dogs and chickens wander freely among the houses while the more valuable pigs are leashed to trees.

Jenicil and Janith spend the morning in the classroom. Both the elementary school and the tiny high school are desperately short of teachers, desks, and books. At lunchtime Jenicil and Janith return home. Two gray and white kittens twine around Jenicil's legs, waiting hopefully for a share of fish and rice.

"*Maayong hapon* [MA-A-yong HA-pon]," Mia calls from the doorway. "Good afternoon." She's here to talk with Digoy.

Digoy lifts a speared filefish into his paddleboat.

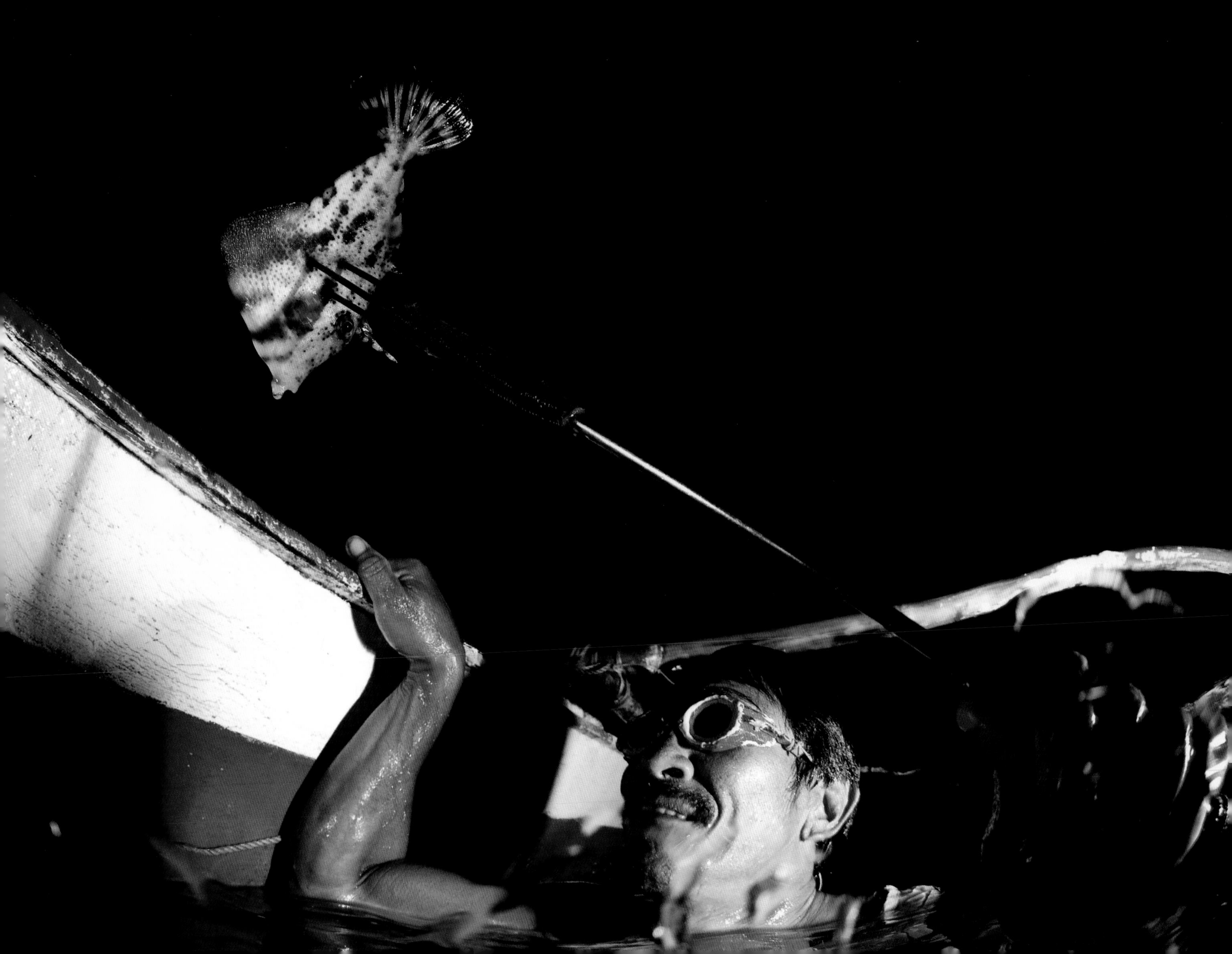

The Paden family at lunch. There is no running water on the island, so the Padens draw their fresh water from a nearby well and store it in plastic jugs.

Mia asks him how much time he currently spends fishing, as well as how many fish he is catching. Digoy patiently answers all her questions. Mia asks him about the MPA. Digoy was one of the MPA's first supporters. Does he still think setting aside part of the reef is a good idea?

"I think it is a good idea because of the illegal fishing," says Digoy firmly. "We need something to protect the fish. Especially the young fish."

Digoy's commitment is very important. Protected areas don't stay protected very long unless people living nearby, such as Digoy, see them as a good thing. The local people are the ones who must guard the reserves and provide the grassroots political support that will keep them closed to fishing.

Jenicil and her sister return to school while their father gets some much-needed sleep. At the end of the day Jenicil sits on the slatted bamboo outside the bedroom to do math homework. Gertrudes calls the family to dinner. As the sun sets, lamps and lanterns are lit in Handumon's homes. There is no electricity in the community. The lack of power restricts the kinds of work people can do on Handumon and limits the time children can spend reading or studying.

Out on the reef the daylight creatures tuck themselves away. The tiger tail seahorses and other nighttime creatures emerge. Digoy says good night to his family and gathers his goggles, fin, spear, and lantern. Cricket song fills the night air as he once again heads into the ink-dark sea.

Jenicil, like children everywhere, has homework to do.

The kerosene lantern on the tip of Digoy's prow lights up the shallow water.

Seahorses and Traditional Chinese Medicine

In Danajon Bank, most seahorse fishers dry the seahorses they catch and sell them to local shopkeepers. Other fishers sell the live seahorses to aquarium traders. Both sets of seahorses eventually end up in Cebu, the biggest city in the central Philippines. From Cebu, the live ones go primarily to the United States, and the dried ones are shipped to China or other countries for use in traditional Chinese medicine. Dried seahorses are ground up, combined with other ingredients, and given to patients suffering from skin ailments, breathing difficulties, or sexual problems. Amanda recognizes that many Chinese rely on traditional medicine, and many Filipino families rely on the money they earn from seahorse fishing. "We are intent on making the seahorse trade sustainable," says Amanda.

"Sustainable trade" means buying or selling something without running out of it or wrecking something else (like a coral reef) along the way. Instead of trying to fight the people who use seahorses in medicine, Amanda asked them for input and advice. "We can listen before we act," she explains.

Amanda found that the Chinese traditional medicine practitioners in Hong Kong—where most dried seahorses from the Philippines end up—didn't want seahorses to disappear any more than she did. After discussions with Project Seahorse, the Hong Kong Chinese Medicine Merchants Association asked its members to limit the use of dried seahorses whenever possible.

Project Seahorse also helped to broker a global agreement (among 175 countries) to limit the seahorse trade to levels that won't threaten wild populations. As part of that agreement, many of the world's

Amanda examines dried seahorses and dried pipefish at a market in Beihai, China.

Dried seahorses for sale. A fisher earns twenty-five pesos (about fifty-two cents) for a large seahorse, fifteen pesos (about thirty-one cents) for a medium-sized seahorse, and ten pesos (about twenty cents) for a small seahorse.

countries have promised not to export (sell to other countries) seahorses smaller than ten centimeters (about four inches) in length.

"This will allow seahorses to get big enough to reproduce, but still allows some fishing," says Amanda. "It's not perfect, but it's a useful tool."

Unfortunately, a poorly written Philippine law interpreted the global agreement as a ban on all seahorse fishing. This law penalizes the fishing communities that were trying to manage seahorse fishing carefully. Meanwhile, the "underground" trade goes on, but nobody is able to track how many seahorses are being fished. Project Seahorse is urging the Philippine government to change the law to allow seahorse populations to be managed responsibly, while imposing bans only where absolutely necessary. Under a legal, controlled seahorse fishery, patients will get medicine, fishers will be able to support their families, and seahorses will not be stripped from the sea.

CHAPTER FIVE

Good Seahorse Neighbors

A tiger tail seahorse in the Handumon MPA. In the wild, seahorses live from one to five years, depending on the species.

Things are changing in Handumon and other villages along Danajon Bank. Although many mangroves have been cut down, new ones are being replanted. Outside the nearby village of Jandayan Sur, a boy climbs into the branches of a mangrove to pluck a shoot that looks like a giant green bean. Other children carry bundles of shoots across the dark, squelching mud and plant them in long rows. Their mothers, fathers, grandmothers, and grandfathers help, too. This village has already replanted thousands of mangrove shoots. Once grown, these mangroves will provide a refuge for young reef animals. And when a storm comes the mangroves will shield the villagers from powerful winds and raging waves.

A boy carries mangrove sprouts to be planted.

Project Seahorse has helped local communities develop thirty-three MPAs along Danajon Bank. One of the newest is in Busali-an. "This used to be the center of illegal fishing in this area," says Heather. "And sometimes at night you still hear a blast in the distance. But now the village council has set aside money to support their MPA."

Although blast-fishing has long been against the law in the Philippines, many people ignored the law. But things are changing. Project Seahorse social workers have helped local fishers develop a system to use donated cell phones to text-message the local police if they spot someone blast-fishing

Mangrove planting is muddy work!

or fishing in a protected area. Respect for the law is an important part of conservation.

Right now much less than 1 percent of the ocean is protected. Every country will need to do better if we want our seas to provide food and enjoyment for all the generations to come. Amanda, Heather, and everyone else at Project Seahorse are doing everything they can to help Danajon Bank become a model for the Philippines and the rest of the world.

When Heather got married a few years ago, she and her husband, Lawrence, urged their wedding guests not to bring presents. Instead, they asked their friends and family to donate money so that a community on Danajon Bank could strengthen its MPA. "It was our gift to the reef, the seahorses, and the people of Busali-an," says Heather.

Heather and Lawrence's decision led to a guardhouse and patrol boat for Busali-an's new MPA. The patrol boat, decorated with blue, red, and yellow flags, floats in the shallows. The guardhouse isn't yet ready, but long poles rising from the water mark the spot where it will soon stand vigil over the reef. Heather is thrilled that the local government chipped in funds for the guardhouse, and that villagers will help build it. When local people invest in a conservation project, it has the best chance of success.

A whitetip reef shark in the Sulu Sea, Philippines. As reefs recover from overfishing, top predators (such as sharks) return. Top predators are a sign of a healthy ocean. The Project Seahorse team hopes that the MPAs created by Handumon, Busali-an, and many other communities will help Danjon Bank regain its natural diversity.

Pink anenomefish live on the Danajon Bank.
Scientists estimate that coral reefs are home
to 4,000 different fish species.

Busali-an celebrates its new marine protected area.

Amanda's daughter Andaya peeks from underneath her mother's sun hat. Amanda so loves this area and its people that she named Andaya after the island of Jandayan, where the village of Handumon is located.

The people of Busali-an welcome Heather, Amanda, and the Project Seahorse team to a dedication ceremony for the new guardhouse. A feast of clams, crabs, fish, fried bananas, mangoes, noodles, green coco-nut, and sticky rice wrapped in palm fronds is spread across a table. The women of Busali-an offer handwoven sun hats and flower necklaces to Heather and Amanda. Heather's daughter Jemima plops Heather's hat on her own head. Amanda's daughter Andaya gets a hat, too.

When Andaya gets sleepy, Amanda sings "Baby Beluga" to her. Amanda says she once watched in wonder as a playful beluga whale at the John G. Shedd Aquarium in Chicago blew

The dedication ceremony for the new Busali-an MPA guardhouse.

Heather and Jemima aboard Busali-an's new patrol boat.

bubble rings and balanced the rings on its head. "I've never felt the same about belugas since," says Amanda, "and I was already in love with ocean life."

After the feast, the ceremony moves to the water. Heather, Jemima, Amanda, and Andaya climb into the new patrol boat. Other bancas follow. Everyone motors out to the spot where the Busali-an guardhouse will be built. As the adults make their speeches, Jemima plucks petals from her mother's flower necklace and drops them into the turquoise water. They drift silently away, dipping and bobbing with the flow of the sea.

Ideas can spread like petals in a current.

More and more people recognize the need to protect our oceans, particularly our beautiful and vulnerable coral reefs. It's not always easy to stop using part of a reef, especially in places where people have few other ways of earning a living. But it's one simple thing we can do today to make sure the seas are healthy tomorrow. And it can help save the seahorse.

Seahorses are just some of the many coral reef residents. But seahorses have a special place in people's hearts. "After all," Amanda says, "a seahorse is the only fish that holds your hand."

Amanda with a tiger tail seahorse.

Onion World

Seahorse conservation—like all conservation—means action on many levels. It begins with seahorse biology and extends outward. First we must consider the seahorse itself; then the coral reef where it lives; then the fisher who catches it; then the local community; then the region, or nation; and then the world. All these levels are important because there is an impact on the seahorse at each level. Amanda calls these layers "the Onion World." Every layer of the onion affects the seahorse clinging to its holdfast. We have to relieve pressure at all layers if we are to help the seahorse at the center of this Onion World.

THE FISH
The seahorse in its home on the reef.

6 5 4 3 2

THE FISHER
Impact on seahorses: The impact depends on whether the fisher targets seahorses, the number and size of seahorses caught, and how the seahorses and other fish are caught (some fishing methods harm the reef).

THE REEF
Impact on seahorses: Seahorses need a healthy reef ecosystem to thrive, including healthy seagrass and mangrove habitats.

2

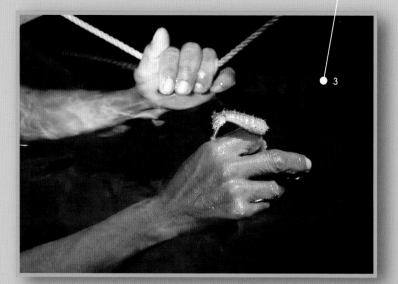

3

THE WORLD

Impact on seahorses: The international demand for seahorses in traditional Chinese medicine, the curio trade, and the aquarium trade encourages seahorse fishing. Global warming threatens reefs. Countries also enter into international agreements to control trade in seahorses and other endangered animals.

THE REGION AND NATION

Impact on seahorses: The regional or national government makes laws governing fishing (including seahorse fishing), may give money for enforcement, and makes decisions about whether or not to create and support MPAs. If a government is well run and honest, its MPAs will have the best chance of success.

THE COMMUNITY

Impact on seahorses: The community depends on the coral reef and mangrove habitats for income, food, and building materials. The community also decides whether or not to support local MPAs, and whether or not to enforce laws against destructive fishing.

51

Glossary

Banca—A Filipino word for a slender wooden boat with outriggers.

Blast-fishing—A very destructive fishing method that uses explosives dropped into water.

Brood—A group of young born at the same time.

Ecosystem—A system formed by a community of organisms interacting with their environment.

Evolve—To develop a characteristic through the process of evolution.

Evolution—Change, from generation to generation, by biological processes, including natural selection (in natural selection, characteristics that help a living thing survive and reproduce are passed on from generation to generation, which over time can result in new species).

Fisher—A person who fishes. (*Fisher* is the internationally accepted replacement for the word *fisherman,* which tends to make people think that only men fish.)

Habitat—The environment in which an animal or plant naturally lives.

Marine Protected Area (MPA)—A part of the ocean that has received formal, lasting protection in order to preserve its natural resources.

Nutrients—Food that is necessary for life, health, and growth.

Overfishing—To take so many fish that the population is depleted or exhausted.

Polyp—A kind of animal that has a mouth, tentacles, and usually a fixed base.

Photosynthesis—A chemical process that harnesses the sun's energy to produce nutrients from air and water.

Predator—An animal that eats other animals.

Sustainable trade—A process of gathering, buying, and selling that does not deplete or exhaust the resource that is being traded.

Transect—A path or line along which a scientist records and counts the object of study.

Acknowledgments

The author and photographer would like to thank the staff of Project Seahorse and its Filipino sister organization, the Project Seahorse Foundation for Marine Conservation, including Amanda Vincent, Heather Koldewey, Jonathan Anticamara, Amado Blanco, Mia Apurado, Pert Auxilio,

Alfie Bartolo, Sarah Bartnik, Reaan Catitig, Mia Comeros, J. R. Dongallo, Nick Hill, Lourdes Labrada, Sara Lourie, Kerrie O'Donnell, Hazel Panes, Marjorie Sorensen, and Franco Villaruel for the time and care they devoted to this project. Their unfailing patience and good company is much appreciated. I am particularly grateful to Amanda Vincent for the many hours she spent reviewing and correcting this manuscript; Kerry O'Donnell also provided valuable feedback. Rodrigo "Digoy" Paden and his family— Gertrudes, Joel, Janith, and Jenicil—were very kind to invite us into their home and allow us a glimpse of their daily lives. The children and teachers of Handumon Elementary School deserve a big thank-you for allowing us to interrupt their school day. We are indebted to the entire Handumon community for their gracious hospitality. The author would also like to thank the people of Busali-an for including her in their MPA dedication celebrations.

As great admirers of marine wildlife, we would like to note that every seahorse photographed for this book was returned unharmed to the reef.

Resources

VIDEO

Blue Planet: Seas of Life. BBC Warner, 2007 **(dsc.discovery.com/tv/blue-planet/ blue-planet.html)**.

Kingdom of the Seahorse. Nova, 1997 **(www.pbs.org/wgbh/nova/seahorse/)**.

Planet Earth ("Shallow Seas" episode). BBC Warner, 2007 **(dsc.discovery.com/convergence/ planet-earth/planet-earth.html)**.

INTERNET

Visit the Project Seahorse website at **www.projectseahorse.org**.

The Coral Reef Alliance offers guides for snorkelers, turtle watchers, and whale watchers: **www.coral.org**.

Monterey Bay Aquarium has special ocean activities for kids at **www.mbayaq.org/lc/kids_place/**.

BOOKS

There are four other Scientists in the Field books about the ocean:

Diving to a Deep-Sea Volcano by Kenneth Mallory. Boston: Houghton Mifflin, 2006.

Swimming with Hammerhead Sharks by Kenneth Mallory. Boston: Houghton Mifflin, 2002.

Tracking Trash: Flotsam, Jetsam, and the Science of Ocean Motion by Loree Griffin Burns. Boston: Houghton Mifflin, 2007.

The Whale Scientists: Solving the Mystery of Whale Strandings by Fran Hodgkins. Boston: Houghton Mifflin, 2007.

A male ribbon eel on a coral reef in Manado, Indonesia.

A weedy seadragon in Australia. Scientists group seahorses within a family that also includes seadragons, pipefishes, and pipehorses.

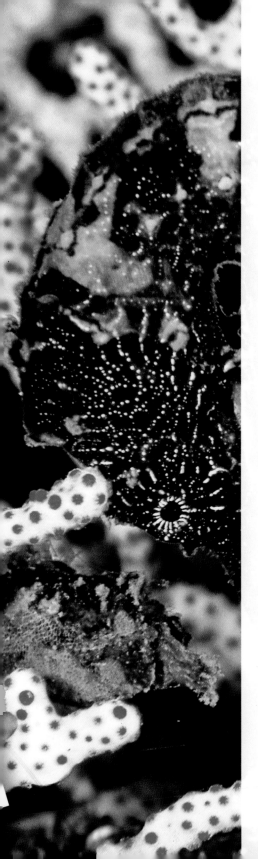

How to Help Seahorses

(This helpful guide is courtesy of Project Seahorse.)

Seahorses are unusual, beautiful fish that people like to keep as pets. Think before you decide to buy a seahorse. They are very difficult to keep alive and healthy, as they eat only live food and are vulnerable to disease.

Even with all your efforts and care your seahorses may die. If they do, please resist the temptation to replace them.

Avoid buying souvenirs and curiosities made from dead seahorses.

Handicrafts with seahorse motifs make great gifts. They can also provide seahorse fishers and their families with an alternative, sustainable source of income.

Observe but do not touch seahorses in the wild, and do not take them out of the water.

Read about seahorses. Look for information about them in books and magazines, on the Internet, and at museums and aquariums.

Send us information about seahorses, because we are learning, too. Let us know if you see seahorses in the wild or for sale in shops. In addition, tell us if you are successfully keeping seahorses in an aquarium.

Encourage others to support seahorse conservation and marine conservation in general. Support projects that work to protect the seagrass, coral, mangrove, and estuarine habitats where seahorses live.

Send a donation to Project Seahorse to fund our work. We also welcome books, posters, maps, videos, slides, and other educational materials to help us teach people about seahorses.

INDEX

Page numbers in bold type refer to photographs or captions.

A pipefish glides over a reef.